Stories From Amish Country

John Schmid

ISBN 13: 9798866035359

Stories

Preface

Country singer Hank Williams said, "A song is three minutes to tell somebody's life story."

A story is a great way to tell a truth; to describe a culture; to preserve history; to entertain a crowd or a family; to help pass the time.

This little book is a collection of some of the stories that I have heard over the years here in Amish Country.

I think I got the idea to put some of these stories in writing after hearing David Kline tell the story of his neighbor who was a Cleveland Indians fan (see chapter 5, "The Preacher Who Ran the Bases"). I got to thinking: *These stories need to be preserved.*

So, here are 20-some true stories that I experienced myself or heard at church or the coffee shop or the sale barn...

This is Volume One. I'm sure there are more stories. So stand by.

John Schmid

We are all storytellers.
We all live in a network of stories.
There isn't a stronger connection between people than
storytelling.

-- Jimmy Neil Smith
Director of the International Storytelling Center

~ 1

Joni Miller's Barn

I WAS BORN and raised in the Wayne-Holmes County area of Ohio, home to lush, green rolling pastures; picturesque frame farmhouses that date back to the early 1800s; and the largest Amish settlement in the world (although it wasn't the largest when I was born). I didn't realize how beautiful this area was until I left home. Now that I'm back, I try not to take the charm and beauty of this area for granted.

It was there that I met and married a sweet young girl by the name of Lydia Byler, who was born into the home of an Amish preacher. By the time I met her, the family had left the Amish church and joined Fairlawn Conservative Mennonite Church, where her dad, Tobias, eventually became the bishop.

Tobias, who went by "Tobe," was born and raised in Wayne County, also a part of this beautiful part of the world. Lydia's mom, Amelia, was from Buchanan County, Iowa. They both grew up in churches that would be called "Swartzentruber" Amish (named after one of their bishops).

The Swartzentruber Church had rightly earned its reputation as the strictest and most no-nonsense group of Amish in the entire country (depending on your definition of *nonsense*).

On the basis of stout religious convictions, it was and still is forbidden to have the worldly influence of indoor plumbing, gravel on your lane, varnish on your hardwood floors, and a window in the back of your buggy. To avoid other vain pretense, this group will not hang lace curtains in their windows. Or even plain curtains that part in the middle. A window covering has to be one solid sheet of cloth. Plain and simple, home-spun, non-split cloth will do just fine to keep the sunlight out by day and the flickering kerosene light inside at night.

Speaking of kerosene, this same group firmly draws the line on exterior illumination as well. Battery-powered lights on their black horse-drawn buggies are forbidden; only vintage kerosene lamps will do. Furthermore, there are no musical instruments allowed in their churches or inside their houses. If a joyful noise needs to be made unto heaven, then natural voices will do just fine, thank you. They sing s-l-o-w, Gregorian-chant-style songs from the *Ausbund*, which is the oldest continuously used Protestant hymnbook in the world. The songs were written mostly by Anabaptists in European prisons.

It goes without saying that Swartzentruber Amish eschew all things electric, including radios, televisions, and the most recent of diabolical creations—the cell phone (though in certain circumstances, pay phones have been permitted).

Some members of this ultra-orthodox Amish group are so strict they do not allow their men to wear shoes from Memorial Day to Labor Day. Though they would agree we all have souls, they see no reason to wear them on our feet during the summer months. A few months of barefoot wear and tear plowing fields or herding cattle in summer temperatures will turn the skin on anyone's feet tough as shoe leather.

You might guess their position on changing to Daylight Savings Time. (They don't.) I'll spare the why, but suffice it to say all you need to know is they rise when the sun does and turn down their covers when it disappears, while toiling as hard as they can in between. That's all the Greenwich Mean Time the Swarztentrubers will ever need.

And even during the sweltering heat of summer, these devout Amish are not supposed to roll up their sleeves. They must wear vests and keep their shirts buttoned all the way to the top and the sleeves all the way to the wrist. These rules may vary from church to church, but you get the point. I won't say much about the dress code for Swarztentruber women, but suffice it to say it's been some time since anyone has accused them of being slaves to fashion.

It was for many of these reasons and perhaps more that my wife's parents decided in the mid-1940s to exit the Swartzentruber Church for a fellowship where the grapes were a little less black.

THE NEWLY MARRIED Byler couple (my future in-laws) and a dozen or so other families made the decision to leave the Swartzentrubers and join the "Abe Troyer" Amish Church, a little less restrictive (emphasis on "little"). The church was called by its bishop's name. They did not just desire to be free of the unbending rules that in many cases did not make sense to them, but they were also on a quest for a deeper connection to God that, for one reason or another, had so far eluded them growing up.

Well, as it turned out, the Abe Troyer Church had its fair share of absolutes as well. It seemed like it was just more of the same. They were not satisfied in this new church either.

One of the families who left with the group was the Joni Miller family. Joni was my father-in-law's first cousin. He lived on a farm on Kidron Road, just a quarter mile south of US route 250. One day as Joni was painting his barn with white paint, bishop Abe Troyer drove by. Spotting Joni hard at work painting his barn, the ever-vigilant bishop immediately pulled up on the reins of his buggy. He carefully steered his sleek horse into the farmyard.

"Greetings, Brother Joni," the bishop said as he brought his team to a halt.

"Greetings, Bishop Troyer," came Joni's polite reply, with a nod of his straw hat. (I'm just guessing at this conversation. He probably said, "Hi, Abe.")

The good bishop, clearing his throat in preparation for delivering what would no doubt come as unwelcome news to the farmer, said in a calm but unmistakably concerned and stern voice, "Brother Joni, don't you realize that in the Abe Troyer church we do not allow anyone to have a white barn? Your barn must be painted red. You cannot have a white barn and be a member of my church."

Joni indeed knew the rules. He also understood that painting his barn white was a punishable offense in the Abe Troyer flock. If not remedied at once, the white barn could lead to church discipline and ultimately ex-communication and the painful shunning by his neighbors.

Joni, sensing a moment that might not come again to make

4

his statement about the suffocating rules he could no longer abide by, smiled politely at the bishop and said,

"Ya, ich vayss." ("Yes, I know.")

With that, Joni turned around, dipped his brush into the bucket of illegal white paint, and splashed a fresh coat of dazzling white pigment over the weathered wood.

I don't know what else was said, but the message had been sent: "We're out of here!"

Not long after that, Cousin Joni sold his farm to his brother-in-law, Mony Mony's Andy, and moved to a more liberal Amish church in the state of Maryland. One where white barns don't necessarily lower your odds for getting into Heaven.

The moral of the story seems to be that some people, when they're upset with a church, quit giving their tithe or they might even choose to raise their voice at a church business meeting. Not so with the gentle Amish.

When you're ready to leave a church, you simply paint your barn white. At least, in the Abe Troyer Church.

I know this story because after Joni sold his farm to Mony Mony's Andy (my wife's uncle) in 1945, Andy then sold the farm to Bill Joe's Josie Miller in 1949. Josie's family and his children are good friends of mine. One day Joni stopped by to visit his old Kidron homestead, and he told the barn-painting story to Josie and those sitting around the table. Josie's son-in-law, Crist Miller, was there and he then told the story to me.

MANY YEARS LATER, when some of the rules had loosened up, Joni, in Oakland, Maryland, was giving his testimony on a conference-type call on what is known as the Amish Chat Line (yes, on a telephone). At the end of his spiritual journey story, he asked if there were any questions.

Crist Miller piped up, "Tell 'em about painting the barn and Abe Troyer!"

"How did you know that?" exclaimed Joni.

Crist reminded Joni that he had been at Josie's place the day Joni stopped in and told the story. So Joni again told the story to everyone (100? 50? people) on the chat line that night. It is no longer a secret.

Post script: At the Amish funeral of a lady who was a cousin to both father-in-law Tobe and cousin Joni, I recounted that story to one of Joni's children. He laughed. He had never heard that particular story, but he did tell me that when his dad moved from Ohio to Maryland, he was so fed up with rules and regulations that he didn't officially join a church for almost a year. He "sat on the fence," the son told me. Then he said that an Amish preacher from Maryland had said, "That's why we changed the rules and allowed electric fences."

~ 2

Be Sure Your Guitar Will Find You Out

AMISH RULES DO not allow musical instruments, except maybe an occasional harmonica, even though many of the Amish had a guitar in their running-around days (*rum-schpringah* days, pronounced, *room* schpringah). Those rules are still in effect, although the rules don't seem to be as strictly enforced as they were in my day.

For a couple of years, I drove a school bus for the East Holmes school district. One morning on my bus route, one of my Amish schoolboys told me the story of his dad's guitar.

When his dad (let's call him "Sam") was young, he secretly bought a guitar. He hid it upstairs and only played it when everyone was gone and the house was empty, as when they all went to Sunday church or to an auction.

And so it was bound to happen sooner or later.

One day Sam got careless and forgot to put his guitar away. He left it lying out in plain sight on his bed. His little brother happened to walk into the room, saw the guitar, and asked, "Sam, what is that thing?"

"Nothing," Sam said, as he quickly stuck the guitar back in its hiding place. (Under the bed? In the closet?) "It's nothing!"

That evening after little brother's discovery, while the Amish family was gathered around the supper table, Sam's little brother wiped his mouth and blurted out, "Dat! Sam hat en box schpiyhah, un es hat droadah druff!" ("Dad! Sam has a box upstairs and it has wires on it!")

Silence filled the room. A very loud silence. Father said nothing but simply looked at Sam, raised his right eyebrow, and motioned for him to bring the contraption on down. Sam made what must have been a long, agonizing climb up the stairs to retrieve the guitar.

Now in these parts, you never know what an Amish father will do when he discovers a guitar. It depends on the local church rules, or on the leniency or strictness of the father. Some may turn it over and over like stolen property and then demand it go back to its original owner. Others may say nothing and just break it over their knee, while still others may choose to add it to the brush pile on the edge of the pasture and let the matter go up in smoke come fall. I know of one mother who put her son's accordion in the wood stove. When her son came downstairs one morning, his mother asked, "Can you smell that music?" Nowadays, there are parents who will just wink and say nothing.

And these are just the peaceable options.

Sam went upstairs and brought the guitar down to his dad.

His father took it from him and examined it carefully. He turned it over a couple of times and stared into the hole in the center of the guitar. Then he looked at the neck, examining the marks and scratches.

"Where did you get this guitar, son?" he asked.

"I bought it from a friend." (Sam paid four dollars for it!)

8

Sam's father turned it over a couple more times and then looked up and stared his son in the eye.

Long pause.

"This was my guitar," he finally said quietly and set it down on the table.

You could have heard a fly buzzing in the barn (or, a pin drop...). The children stared at their father in wide-eyed disbelief. None of them had the slightest idea that their faithful, strict Amish dad had once played the guitar himself.

What are the chances of an Amish boy selling his guitar, joining church, getting married, having children, and then 20-some years later, his son purchasing that same guitar from a friend?

That was as much of Sam's story as his son told me at the time. Toward the end of the summer, I ran into Sam's son again and asked, "Hey, whatever happened to your dad's guitar?"

"Grandpa said he could keep the guitar." He smiled. "But it must stay in the house. He said there would be no playing in public. Period."

Just recently, I told the story at the local coffee shop, and someone turned around and said, "I hear Sam is playing guitar again. And he's pretty good."

Not long after that, I was at an auction and I met Sam. Although we are the same age and would have run around at the same time, I don't remember ever actually meeting him.

"You're the guitar man!" I teased. He smiled and without saying a word showed me his fingers. They were calloused on the ends. From playing guitar.

So when it comes to guitars, there is something of an

unspoken truce in our community. I'm often asked to play at school fundraisers and local events, and when I do there will often be Amish in the back, serving food and selling quilts. Technically speaking, they can tell the bishop they didn't come to hear me play. They were just minding their own business, and I happened to be on the stage singing.

Once in a while the truce will break down and I'll be disinvited to an event. As one man told me, "John, we're going to have to cancel you. We're having a little trouble in our church, so it might be better if there's no guitar at our event."

I politely say, "I understand." Which I do.

The times have changed quite a bit in the Amish culture concerning music. I remember parents coming to me 40 years ago and lamenting, almost with tears, "My son is playing guitar!"

"I'm so sorry," I would try to convey, without actually lying.

Now, a parent will confide with a touch of pride, "My son is playing guitar!"

Last summer I was at a fund raiser where a local "Amish" band was playing. These were young musicians who had not yet joined the church. A man standing beside me leaned over and elbowed me and said with a smile, "That's my son on the drums!"

I'm still looking for a chance to jam with Sam. I wonder if he still has his dad's guitar.

ONE MORE MUSIC story:

Willard Graber hosts music concerts in his yard on the corner of Kaufman and Birky Streets in Pinecraft, Sarasota, Florida. Pinecraft is a small section of Sarasota occupied mostly by Amish and Mennonites who come to Florida during the winter. Willard's yard has become known as "Birky Square." I call it the Carnegie Hall of Pinecraft. Concerts there have drawn crowds of over 1,000 people squashed together in the yard and spilling out into the streets. Drive slow when there is concert there!

While I was singing there one night, a friend of mine was in the back of the crowd. As he looked around the scene, his eyes caught the eyes of the Amish man standing beside him, so he teased him with a question.

"Does your bishop know you're here, listening to this music?"

"I am the bishop," was the man's simple reply.

~ 3

Amos Flunks His Driver's Test

ONE OF JAKE Graber's granddaughters was getting married. At the wedding celebration in Jamesport, Missouri, the Graber family was telling stories of some of the characters of their childhood. Since most of the people in the story are long gone, I will use their real names. Well, at least their real nicknames.

HIS REAL NAME was Amos, but everyone called him "Amy-boy." His dad's nickname was Simple Johnny, if that gives you any insight into the community's opinion of their intellectual abilities.

Simple Johnny and his family were Amish, but Amy-boy had a little of a renegade spirit in him and he got himself a radio, which in turn got him into a little bit of trouble with the powers that be. News that Amy had a radio called for a visit by the preachers. In many churches, a pastoral call is a blessing, but in the Amish church, a visit by the preachers usually means something is out of order: rules have been broken, someone is sick, there's a financial crisis...

The preachers let Amy-Boy know that they knew he had a radio. Amy-Boy didn't say much at first, but as rebellious as he may be, he wasn't going to lie. After a few questions and nudgings, Amos realized that he was caught. He finally confessed that yes, he did happen to own a radio.

The preachers asked if he would go get it so they could properly dispose of it. Amy-boy turned to his little brother and said, "Go get the radio."

Little brother, anxious to be as helpful as he could, said, "Okay, Amy. The big one or the little one?"

ONE DAY, AMOS decided he was going to get a car, a gas machine, even though that too was strictly against the church rules.

He went to town and filled out all the papers and studied the booklet about traffic laws, and when he took the written test, he was pleased to discover that he had passed. Barely. But he now had his driver's permit.

Amy-boy didn't have a lot of experience driving one of these mechanical contraptions, but how hard could it be? Left foot, clutch; right foot, gas pedal and brake. On the back roads of Hicksville, Ohio, Amy-boy drove his English friend's car up and down the gravel roads until he pretty much had this modern gas machine mastered. It was almost easier than a horse and buggy.

A week later, Amy-boy went to town to take the actual driving test.

He and the officer climbed into the borrowed car and took off.

"Turn right on Main Street," the officer said.

"Turn left on Maple."

Left and right they went, up one street and down the other.

Then back to Main Street.

Amy-boy was doing fairly well in this driver's test until he came to the last traffic light. It was red. But instead of stopping, he drove right through the red light. With the officer sitting right beside him!

"What are you doing?" yelled the officer as they sped down Main Street. "Didn't you see that red light?"

"Yes, I did, but didn't *you* see that Amish man walking down the sidewalk?"

THAT WAS THE end of the story as the living room full of Grabers roared with laughter, even though they had heard the story numerous times. Amy-boy flunked his first driver's test. I never did hear if he tried again and finally got his license. That didn't seem to be an important issue to the telling of the story.

~ 4

Bema Dan's Roy and Junie

BEMA DAN'S ROY is a musician. He is ten years older than I am, so when I was just starting to play guitar, he was one of our heroes. I never really knew him, but his reputation was legendary among us young musicians. He played in Nashville for some famous country music stars: Elvis, Johnny Cash, Porter Wagoner...

About the only time I ever actually talked to Roy was at a movie house in Wooster one night when Mahlon Detweiler and I went to a movie (a rare occasion) and Roy was taking the tickets. Mahlon was our guitar player and he knew Roy.

"Hey, I hear you guys are really doing well with your band. Keep it up!" Roy said as we gave him our tickets and headed for the popcorn stand. What a compliment! And from a Nashville musician! I floated on into the movie house.

Through the years, we discovered that Roy may have embellished the facts just a tad. He may not have *actually* played for Elvis. Or Cash. He probably just went to one of their concerts. Or he was in the same town. The fact is, he was a pretty good musician and played with a band. He was still a hometown hero.

I saw Roy when he came home from Cincinnati to attend

his sister's Amish funeral. I didn't realize Bill Mary and he were siblings until I read the obituary.

I saw him across the room where the funeral was being held, in Bill Mary's nephew's shop across the road from the Bema Dan home farm. I would not have recognized him. I hadn't seen him for 40-some years, and I had never really known him personally. I was anxious to talk to him and see if he even knew who I was. I wanted to tell him how he inspired us young musicians, even if he didn't *actually* play for Elvis (but I wasn't going to tell him that).

After the funeral, everyone was standing around asking each other if they were going to the graveyard. It was just over the hill, and the pallbearers would not even load the coffin in a buggy; they carried it the whole way up the hill, about 100 yards.

I saw Roy surrounded by nephews and old neighbors, and I stood around for about five minutes, waiting my turn. Then I decided to go to the graveyard and talk to Roy there or afterward at the meal.

We gathered up the hill at the graveyard and stood around as the family watched the coffin being lowered into the ground and the four young Amish men carefully shoveled dirt on and around the coffin, slowly filling up the grave. I kept looking around for Roy. After a while, I asked people if he was there.

"Have you seen Roy?"

"Oh, he won't come to the graveyard. He probably won't even hang around to eat. You'd better go back down to the shop and talk to him before he leaves."

I left the gravesite and hurried right back down to the shop, but it was too late. Roy had already left.

"He never hangs around very long," someone told me. "He comes to Amish family services late and leaves early."

Bummer.

Tom Miller, a local excavator and neighbor of the Bema Dan family, was at the funeral. He and I had arranged to leave the funeral and go to the Plum Run Cemetery in northeast Holmes County to straighten up and repair the heavy tombstone of my great-great grandparents. So after lunch and after visiting with many people we hadn't seen for a while, I jumped in Tom's truck and with the track hoe on the trailer, we headed to Plum Run Cemetery, about 40 minutes away.

As we drove the 25 miles, we got to talking about Roy, and I learned that there are a lot of "Bema Dan's Roy" stories. Of the many Tom told in that half hour, here is my favorite:

TOM'S UNCLE JUNIE Schlabach lived in Shreve for a number of years in the '70s. He owned several businesses, including the laundromat, the car wash, and the Shreve Hotel. His boyhood friend, Roy, lived in one of Junie's hotel rooms for a few years. You would think that a Nashville musician would have better accommodations, but maybe the rumors of his exaggerations were true.

One day another longtime friend, Alvin Yoder, who also had moved from the Berlin area to Shreve, told Junie that he had a beloved dog that was old and sick and suffering. Could he come and put it out of its misery? Alvin just didn't have the heart to get rid his old faithful dog.

So Junie went out to Alvin's farm and Roy went with him.

19

"Take him out in the field where I can't see him. Shoot him and bury him. I don't want to be near," said Alvin.

Junie and Roy tied the dog up and led him out to a field and around the corner and tied him to a fence post. Junie raised his 20-gauge shotgun and fired, and the dog went to dog heaven with no more than a split second of pain.

What neither Junie nor Roy knew was that a cat was hiding in the high weeds in this corner of the field fence. When the gun went off and before old Shep even hit the ground, the cat jumped four feet straight up in the air! It scared the daylights out of Junie and Roy. When the cat came down his feet were already moving and he ran head long into the fence. BAM! He backed up. WHAM! again, ran right into the fence. He was almost more scared than Roy and Junie, if that were possible.

Junie and Roy laughed so hard they could hardly stand up. In fact, Roy fell to the ground, laughing and holding his stomach, rolling around in the weeds.

Alvin had heard the shot and then noise of human voices. He couldn't tell if it was laughter or screams of despair, and he looked out the window. There was Roy, rolling around on the ground, his face contorted, holding his stomach!

"Oh, Lord!" Alvin cried. "Junie shot Roy!"

Alvin about had a heart attack himself. He ran down to help Roy, and when he learned what had happened, he joined them in uproarious laughter. He got over the grief of the death of his dog in a hurry.

A WEEK OR so after Tom told me this story, I went into Boyd &

Wurthmann Restaurant in Berlin and saw Junie Schlabach sitting at the counter. I went over to him and said something like, "Hey, Junie, I hear that you have a ministry of shooting dogs for neighbors."

He looked up at me sort of stunned and confused, and then burst into uproarious laughter. What a great story!

~ 5

The Preacher Who Ran the Bases

IT WOULD BE fair to say that as a boy growing up in Ohio, I was mesmerized by the Cleveland Indians. Now, the fact they had won only two World Series championships since the franchise was established in 1901 (1920 and 1948) and I wasn't around for either one didn't faze me in the least.

The Amish are theologically and categorically opposed to playing organized competitive sports. This includes such cherished national pastimes as football, basketball, and of course the other love of my life (besides Lydia), Cleveland Indians baseball. Among other reasons, the Amish see sports as a hopelessly frivolous, unjustified waste of time and an unhealthy cause of strife. And it doesn't produce a single bushel of corn, to boot. They'll participate in casual sports among themselves, but professional or interscholastic, organized sports are not approved of by the church. This prohibition even includes *listening* to Major League Baseball, especially if you have a forbidden transistor radio, or nowadays, a cell phone.

Well, I remember the day I pulled into the driveway of David Kline's family. They were hosting an exchange student from Texas. I knew the Texas student's family, so I stopped in to see how she was doing up here in Yankee territory. This Texas girl had not only landed in a different culture coming to Ohio, but staying with the Kline family had also put her in the subculture of the Amish and Pennsylvania Dutch.

I had the radio cranked up, listening to the play-by-play of a Cleveland Indians game by the best announcer in baseball, Tom Hamilton. David was sitting on the porch, and he got up and ambled toward me.

As he reached the window of my car, he heard the radio announcer's excited voice.

"So, you like the Cleveland Indians, hey John?"

"Yes, sort of," I sheepishly replied.

David grinned and began to tell me about his former neighbor just down the road who also loved baseball—and especially the Cleveland Indians.

This neighbor boy Yost was from the strictest order of Amish, the Swartzentruber branch, but he always knew the Cleveland Indians' schedule, the score, the batting averages, the ERAs, the won-lost record, who is starting pitcher tomorrow…

I don't know how he knew all this. The Amish don't have television or radio. In those days, most Swartzentruber Amish didn't even get the newspaper, and if they did, they subscribed by mail, which meant the paper always arrived a day late. He might have heard news at the weekly livestock auction or the local feed mill, but my guess is he got his news the way most of my Amish friends did at that time: the milk truck driver.

The farmers all sold their milk in cans, and the milk truck came to pick up the cans every other day except Sunday. It was against Amish convictions to allow someone to pick up their milk

24

on the Lord's Day (it was work). So on Saturday, most Amish farmers separated the milk from that day, fed the skim milk to the hogs, and made butter from the cream. So even with the milk truck, Indians news was sporadic. But Yost always knew, somehow.

When Yost was around 18 years old, he joined the Amish church. Eighteen is the average age for an Amish boy to "get serious" and be baptized and become a bona fide, certified, authentic member of the church. Settle down, get married, have children, become a responsible church member and citizen of the church community. And quit being interested in baseball! No more of that idle, inconsequential, trivial pursuit of worldly diversions known as major league baseball. No more hours glued to the secret radio. No sirree…

But! Yost still seemed to know the score, the batting averages, the pitcher's ERA, the won-lost record, the starting pitcher each day…

Then, a few years after joining church, Yost was chosen by lot to be a preacher.

Time out: "Chosen by lot." That's how Amish preachers are chosen. By lot. It's a long story, but all the members "vote" by telling the bishop who they think would be fit and qualified to be a preacher, and any man who gets three votes (or two, or four, depending on the church district) is put in the "lot." On a given Sunday, all the chosen men, usually four or five (but I've heard up to a dozen men could be in the lot), are lined up, sitting on a bench up front. Each one chooses one of the hymn books that have been placed on a table in front of the congregation. Then the bishop takes each book from each man, one by one, and opens it in front of the man and the whole congregation. Many congregations tie a string around the book, and the bishop ceremoniously unties the string and slowly and dramatically opens the book. One of the books contains a piece of paper with a scripture written on it, and the man who has picked that book is the new preacher. He is ordained right there, on the spot. He comes to church a regular member and goes home a preacher! For the rest of his life!

Now… Where was I? Oh! Our baseball-loving Amishman who became a preacher. By lot. And even though he was now a preacher, he still seemed to know all the stats of the Indians.

Not long after being ordained, Yost moved to Harmony, Minnesota (an apt name for a community of peace-loving Amish). And as you might guess, just as in Ohio, there is no baseball allowed in the Land of 10,000 Lakes for the Amish, though young boys have been known to play a secret game or two out in the pasture using manure piles for the bases—it gives a whole new meaning to sliding into home.

In Minnesota, Yost was chosen by lot to be a bishop, another step up the hierarchy of authority in the church. Bye-bye Indians forever!

By now I was sitting on the porch with David Kline. He went on to tell me that several years ago his nephew, who is a truck driver, had a load of goods that went through Minnesota not far from Harmony, where Bishop Yost lived. So he pulled off Interstate 90 and drove south 20 miles or so to visit his old neighbor. The two had a great time over coffee, visiting and catching up and talking about the differences between Ohio and Minnesota in landscape and people and churches.

In the course of the conversation, David's nephew asked, "Do you still follow the Cleveland Indians?"

"No! Of course not!" Yost said, as if to say, *You know better than that! What kind of question is that? I'm a Swartzentruber bishop!*

"Well," said the truck-driving nephew, "it's just as well. The Indians aren't very good this year. They have lost nine games in a row!"

The bishop paused just a second, and before he could stop himself, he blurted out, "Ya, but they won last night!"

I TOLD THAT story for several years after I heard it from David Kline. I even called Jake and Lizzie Hershberger, some ex-Amish friends who live in Harmony and asked, "Do you know Bishop Yost?"

"Yes, he was our bishop when we were Amish. Why?"

Then I spilled the beans on the bishop and told them the story. They laughed.

Word got back to Yost that some English guy was telling his story, and then word got back to me that Yost wanted to meet this guy (ahem... me.) And I wanted to meet this legend. He sounded like a different kind of Swartzentruber bishop. I mean, I guess he was a different kind. I really didn't know any Swartzentruber bishops to compare him to. But I decided that the next time I went close to Harmony, I was going to stop at Jake and Lizzie's and get them to introduce me to Bishop Yost.

Sadly, that meeting will never happen. Bishop Yost Hershberger and one of his sons tragically died in a house fire on

New Year's Eve, 2016. Up until his death, I had never used his name in public. I didn't want to betray a confidence, even though all his neighbors probably knew the story.

Lizzie Hershberger sent me the newspaper article about Yost's death. I felt like I had lost a friend, even though I had never met him. I posted his story and his name on Facebook, and shared the story that David Kline had told me.

If you are familiar with Facebook, you know that when something is "posted," there is a place for comments. Among the many comments of sympathy and sadness and promises to pray for the family, there was this comment from a Mark Weaver: "I was that truck driver."

The truck driver! I didn't know Mark, but I knew his brother, Jerry, who was just down the street in Pinecraft, Florida, where I was visiting at the time. I walked over to Jerry's house.

"Hey, you are David Kline's nephew!"

"Yes, I am."

"Your brother is a truck driver!"

"Yes."

"He visited Yost Hershberger in Minnesota."

Oh, yes, Jerry knew Yost Hershberger, their old neighbor. He had heard of his tragic death. He mourned with all who knew Yost. Jerry went on to tell this story about Yost as a young man:

"One day, the neighborhood Amish boys were playing baseball in the pasture. Yost was playing, even though his church district frowned on playing, even if it was with other Amish boys in the pasture with a pile of cow manure as second base.

"Yost was a good athlete. The pitcher fired the ball to Yost and he smacked a line drive into left field. A double for sure. But

28

instead of making the turn at first base and digging for second, he hit first base and kept running straight out into right field!

"The dumbfounded players on both teams watched as Yost ran 100 feet past first base and dived under a haystack. Their confused looks turned to knowing smiles as they heard the *clip clop* and rumble of a Swartzentruber buggy rattling down the road and past the field."

Yost was safe. Under the haystack. No "spies" had seen him!

The moral of the story? A single beats a shunning any day! If you're Amish, be sure your batting average will find you out.

THE YOST STORIES were many. Here's one more:

On October 29, 2020, I went to the viewing (calling hours) of Emma Hilty Shetler. I had pretty much grown up with her husband and her. At the viewing, I met Andy Miller from Ashland. We got to talking about places and people and relatives, and since my wife has cousins in almost every Amish settlement in America, I mentioned the one cousin of hers that I knew in Ashland, and yes, Andy knew her... and her dad, and her brothers, ad infinitum. Which somehow brought us to the totally unrelated story of Yost Hershberger and his love for baseball.

Andy, from Ashland, had gone to school with Yost. I told him the "nine games in a row" story and Andy had a Yost Hershberger story of his own. As he told it:

Skinny Abe was the teacher at Frease School, an Amish school east of Fredericksburg on Frease Road. He was a good teacher, and the Amish school board asked him if he would mind temporarily transferring to Brown School, up on Moreland Road north of Fredericksburg. That school had some rough boys and the teacher had lost control. Maybe Abe could help restore order. Amish boys can be unruly!

So Abe went to Brown School and sure enough, the place was out of control. For two weeks, Abe couldn't (or didn't) do much to change the culture. He taught in the midst of disrespect and interruptions and noise, until one day one of the boys was so disruptive that Abe walked back to his desk and with no expression of anger or dismay on his face, simply grabbed the boy by the hair (remember, Amish boys have a lot of hair in a "bowl cut") and almost lifted him out of his seat.

I don't know how long he held him there or what he did next, but Andy said everything got so quiet you could hear a pin drop. He said from that moment on, order was restored; everyone obeyed and respected the teacher, and soon Abe went back to teaching at Frease School and the former female teacher was reinstated at Brown School.

Fast forward 45 years: A group of local Amish were traveling to Iowa. At the bus station in Chicago, this local group saw another group of Amish from Minnesota. They of course began talking and comparing notes and finding out where everyone was from and who was related to whom, and in the course of the conversation, one of the out-of-state men mentioned that he was originally from Ohio and he went to Brown Amish School in Wayne County. One of the local ladies said, "I also went to Brown School!" and she mentioned a few incidents, including the story about a substitute teacher who grabbed one of the rowdy boys by the hair and held him until everything got deathly quiet.

"We never had any trouble after that," she said.

The Minnesota man, who happened to be a preacher, looked at the lady in disbelief and said, "That teacher was Skinny Abe, and the boy he grabbed by the hair was me!"

"What is your name?" she asked.

"Yost Hershberger," the astounded Amish man said.

Thank you, David Kline, Jerry Weaver, and Andy Miller for these stories. Some of the details are probably not quite accurate, but the gist of the story is true. These men can correct me when they read this.

~ 6

Hello, Couch!

MARVIN AND ERMA Hershberger were in Charm. Marvin went into the Charm Store while Erma waited in the buggy at the hitching rail. As she was waiting, a baseball-loving neighbor pulled his buggy in right beside her. She didn't tell me his name, so I'll call him "Joe," but everyone knew he was a Cleveland Indians fan.

Joe jumped out of his buggy and quickly tied the lead rope to the hitching rail, then almost ran over to the newspaper box and shoved a quarter into the slot, jerked open the cover, and grabbed a newspaper.

Erma said he ripped the paper open to the sports page as he walked to the store entrance. Then he stopped in his tracks and stared at the page. In a few seconds, he furiously crumpled the whole paper into a balled-up mess, threw it into his buggy, and stomped into the store.

Conclusion: The Indians lost last night.

This Indians fan "Joe" and Yost Hershberger were not so untypical in that they were Cleveland Indians fans. Even though organized, competitive, professional sports are not approved of in the Amish Church, many a fan in the Amish communities keeps abreast of all the daily news of our Cleveland team.

Andy is one of those fans.

Andy's nickname is Crazy Benny. Not because he's mentally disturbed, but because he's such a fun-loving and, yes, "crazy" Amishman, who every now and then bends the rules just a bit. Bends?! Ignores!

So when an athletic, former competitive-organized-sports-playing, non-church-member, Amish boy finally does join the church, sometimes it's hard to totally cease and desist from any interest in such worldly matters. That was Benny (and one thousand others).

But at least Benny didn't openly approve of baseball. His wife was a very sincere (read: *strict*) church member, and she would never approve of her husband paying attention to professional baseball. So Benny went underground.

He could keep up with any baseball talk at the sale barn or other places where crowds might gather and discuss typical Amish interests such as horses, corn prices, timber prices, and... baseball. The Amish don't have TV or radio or even electricity. And the newspaper was always a day late. So it was a mystery how Benny knew so much about the Indians.

Here's the secret: Every night before going to bed, Benny would make one last trip to the barn to check on the livestock, make sure the gates were properly latched and all the animals had been fed, no lanterns had been left burning, and... check on the Indians game.

Back behind a 2x8 plank, between the wall and the plank, Benny would reach down and pull up a little transistor radio, turn a switch, hold it up to his ear, and listen long enough to get the score and the inning of the game. And maybe listen to an inning or two. He carefully put the radio back in its secure hiding place and went into the house and went to bed.

One night on his nightly state-of-the-barn trip, he reached down into the darkness between the wall and the plank for his radio and... it wasn't there! He flailed his hand around, back and forth, up and down, but... nothing but air.

He looked up into the darkness and muttered, "Hello, couch!"

He went back into the house, knowing that she knew.

"It was pretty quiet in bed," Benny said. "Then, we had council church." (A yearly Amish church service where all the rules are discussed).

Benny shared this story with Mt. Hope Auction owner Steve Mullet, and his description of finding no radio in his hiding place tells us everything: "Oh, Steve, what a feeling! What a feeling!"

~ 7

They Traded Rocky Colavito!

MY GOOD FRIEND Ivan Yoder told me about the first time he was allowed to plow with a team. He was ten years old, and his dad figured he was old enough and mature enough to handle two horses and a one-bottom plow.

Ivan was plowing in the field when he noticed the milk truck in the barnyard, picking up their cans of milk. The milk truck not only provided milk-hauling service, but many times the driver was their source of news.

The milk truck pulled out and was barely out on the road when Ivan saw his brother Abe (who was also known as "Nooky") rounding the corner of the barn and heading straight for Ivan and the team.

The way he was running, there was obviously some important news, but Nooky was far enough away that Ivan couldn't tell if was good news or bad news. All he could decipher was that it was IMPORTANT news! You don't run that fast for ordinary stuff.

As Nooky got closer, it didn't look good. His face was serious and it looked like he was trying not to cry. It's obviously bad news. Somebody died. Somebody's barn burned down.

There's been a tragedy somewhere. Ivan braced himself.

"Whoa!" said Ivan, and the horses stopped.

About ten feet from the plow, Nooky stopped and blurted out, "They traded Rocky Colavito!"

Ivan sat there on the plow seat, stunned. Traded Rocky Colavito? The backbone of the Cleveland Indians team? The possible home run leader this year? (He tied for second place in home runs that year with 42.) The most popular player on the team? *Traded?*

That was 1959. Sixty-four years ago as of this writing. Real Indians fans are still not over it. General Manager Frank Lane should be in jail. "Trader Frank" became "Traitor Frank."

I heard an interview with Rocky Colavito several years ago. He said that trade was the worst day of his life. It was opening day, and the Indians were playing the Detroit Tigers. Just before the game, Colavito was told, "Not so fast, Rocky! Don't put that Indians uniform on. You're wearing a Tigers uniform today!"

That was how he was informed of his trade. Instead of playing in front of his many fans at home on opening day, he was playing for the visiting team! During the interview I heard on the radio, he never used Frank Lane's name. He referred to Lane only as *that man.*

As I finish writing this chapter in August 2023, Rocky Colavito is in the news because he just celebrated his 90th birthday last week (August 10, 2023). He was 25 years old when Traitor Frank pulled off the stupidest trade in Major League history.

You don't think it was the stupidest trade? Then you're not an Indians fan. You don't think it was the worst trade? Talk to Nooky. Talk to me. We'll educate you.

I went to Nooky's house this week to get permission to use his name and tell his story. He had forgotten some of the details of that tragic day, but he sure did remember the feeling.

"It still hurts," he said.

Leroy's Ball Game

This true baseball story was written by Leroy Kuhns of Fredericksburg, Ohio, and was first published in his "Life on the Farm" column in the Amish magazine *The Connection,* in September 2005.

THIRTY-FIVE YEARS ago, my young 8-year-old mind possessed little knowledge beyond the happenings of our farming neighborhood. My idols of late summer were the members of our threshing ring. I'd watch in awe as the heavy-muscled teenage boys and grown men would perform the task of threshing our wheat and oats. Strenuous manual labor was viewed as a healthy, moral duty that would bring its reward in due time.

What excited me most was that threshing was viewed simply as... a way of having fun. There would be contests of seeing who could haul the biggest load of grain sheaves. Or put a whole shock (7 sheaves) onto the wagon with one pitch of the fork. Too many broken fork handles had a way, though, of bringing on a lecture from the older farmers of the ring.

And then there would be water fights. These would be

performed with no rules or regulations whatsoever. Most any bucket that would hold water was considered usable artillery. I recall one of the more aggressive water fights when Abe Troyer and John J. C.'s Harry Yoder got into a one-on-one battle while they were still the young 'uns of the ring. This particular water fight occurred at our farm, at a time when I was still too young to participate. At the time we had a five-gallon bucket stationed at the end of our cow stable to serve as a commode, in the event of a cow having to urinate while in the stable.

Well, one of the boys considered this bucket fair game and used it to dip water out of one of our barn troughs, which was in need of a thorough cleaning. Meeting his opponent at a barn corner, he rinsed his foe down with the murky water, which contained a tinge of the rancid smelling "salt water"!

In later years, once I was old enough to be involved with the threshing ring, the water fights had kind of subsided. But we still would have our share of fun activities to balance the demanding part of threshing.

John Yoder Jr. and yours truly were now the teenage help of the ring. Most of the time we would be talking about the upcoming trapping season. The balance of our conversation while threshing was mostly about playing overhand fast pitch with a baseball.

Most of the former thresher boys had grown up and moved out of the neighborhood, but a now-married man, Abe Troyer remained. And although his hair was starting to show some gray, he would listen in on our fast pitch talk and occasionally give his opinion on the finer points of the subject.

Then one day while threshing at our farm, as John Jr. and I

left the table immediately after lunch for the shade tree of our front lawn, I noticed Abe coming out of our basement right on my heels. I turned around to face him, and he said, "OK, yo' little Gaylord. Get yourself a ball and glove, gimme a bat, and come out behind your buggy shed and we'll see if you can strike me out."

And thus it was, whenever we would have a few minutes of break time, such as a temporary breakdown of the threshing machine or a rainout, we would grab a piece of lumber, which could vary anywhere from ten inches to two feet in length, to serve as home plate. With a bat, glove, and baseball our needs were met for us to be "at it"—the recreation part of neighborhood labor.

A multiple-factor boundary line cuts through our threshing ring. Our farm was at the south end of the ring. We belonged to a different school and church district. And in my late teens and early twenties, I spent a lot of time playing fast pitch with the boys of Fryburg.

Thus a rivalry was born. While threshing, Abe would call us the "Fryburg Windsplitters." To which I commented that our team could beat any team he would be able to scratch together. This set us up for a regular event of fast pitch on Wednesday evening from July through early September for several years. The games were played at what we then called Elm Grove School. It was a parochial (Amish) schoolground in the center of our threshing ring.

This was 20 to 25 years ago [around 1990], and I'm now amazed how everybody would find a few hours' time each week from their busy schedule to play ball at Elm Grove. We would try

43

to be there by seven o'clock, play until dark, then sit around and visit yet for a spell. This could be quite interesting in itself, with players from 4 or 5 different threshing rings involved with the ball game. Weekly farm news was aired concerning the condition of the crops, the weather, and politics.

Who would win the ball games, you ask? The Fryburg team! Or at least, that's the way I remember it. For some reason I have a hard time remembering the times we lost. (For you Elm Grovers reading this, just calm down... if you want your side of the story told, write your own article.)

With few players accustomed to playing with an official baseball, we switched, for safety's sake, to a hard rubber ball that had a rubber seam. At this particular time, Kellogg's Corn Flakes cereal had a sales promotion offer on their large boxes of corn flakes: 3 box tops would get you a free hard rubber baseball! This was the ideal ball for our needs. But I had a hard time convincing my parents and sister that we all needed to go on a cornflake diet. It seemed like I had to eat corn flakes forever till I'd get a free ball. Both teams relied heavily on the Pete Miller boys to bring a fresh supply of balls each Wednesday evening. With 5 boys on the cornflake diet, they kept the UPS delivery man busy bringing them free baseballs.

Our Fryburg team consisted mostly of prime-aged players, whereas Elm Grove had a mix of young prospects and seasoned old timers. Their hurlers were veterans: Abe Troyer and Melvin Weaver Jr., Lonnie Weaver and his brother Steven, John Yoder Jr., and occasionally Henry N's Dean rounded out their brass of young pitchers. Also on their team were brothers Jerry and Marion Miller; Ura Troyer's Lee; Al Coblentz, which was a pleasure for a pitcher (me) with control problems. I offered a huge strike zone. And David Kline, who had a talent for bringing out the flavor of the whole event.

The Fryburg lineup had Pete's Merv as a right-hand control type pitcher. Then there was his brother, Pete Jr., who was the only southpaw for either team. (A big plus to be the only lefty.) Davey Mike's David would occasionally pitch, and I myself would take my turn on the mound. I relied on two pitches: a hard fastball, and if I got me in trouble, I'd try my other pitch: a faster fastball. Any effectiveness that I had was mostly due to the fact that my control was generally terrible at best, and few hitters dug in on me.

Rounding out our team was Allen Stutzman, Milan Raber (in the early years); my brother, Levi; Davy Mike's Vernon; Dan L's boys: Marvin and David; and infrequently, Jonas E. Miller and Mose L. Miller.

Often there would be a small collection of spectators. Not the behind-the-fence partyers type, but the too-young and the old-timers. I can still picture old E.C. (Elmer Coblentz) pulling his blue pickup truck with his livestock trailer in tow in off the road behind the home plate backstop. And when his step-nephews, Jerry or Marion Miller were at bat, E.C. could be heard cheering them on. "Come on, you coon hunters, show 'em how you can run!"

Of all the games, the one I remember best was one night while Pete Merv was pitching. I was catching, and it was the bottom of the last inning. We (Fryburg) were ahead by several runs. Already at the beginning of the inning, it was too dark to be playing, but I knew Elm Grove wouldn't acknowledge defeat unless we got another three outs. Mervin quickly put the first two batters down. By now the clouded western horizon was fast bringing on total darkness. Players from both teams aggressively objected to us pitching to another batter. We only needed one more out, and I was determined to get it. Every player seemed to be saying, "It's no way safe anymore!" Rising up from behind home plate, I raised my hand in protest.

"OK," I said, "only one more batter. We'll be extra careful and I'll practically guarantee that nobody will get hurt." It was now so dark that I, being the catcher, had to call balls and strikes myself. Our ump lacked proper gear for playing in the dark.

I ran out to the mound and said, "Okay, Merv, here's the plan: You go through your full motion, and so will I, but don't you dare throw the ball. We'll try to strike the batter out without throwing the ball."

"O-KEE-DOKEE," said Merv, with a mischievous grin. "I'll do it."

Back behind home plate now, I checked to see who was batter up. It was Jerry Miller, a soft-spoken, left-handed hitter. He stepped into the batter's box. Once Jerry was all set, Merv rocked and fired. I held off for a second, then smacked my fist in my mitt.

"S-t-r-i-k-e one!"

I heard a few grumbles from the Elm Grove bench. Someone remarked, "They're using a dirty ball on purpose. It's hard to see."

I now noticed several of their players taking position behind the backstop, apparently to check on my honesty for calling balls and strikes. Jerry's face showed nothing but confusion as he lowered his stick. But then as I rose up and went through the motion of throwing the ball out to the mound, Jerry again got set and ready in the batter's box.

Again Merv rocked and fired and upon the "smack" of my mitt, I called out "S-t-e-e-r-i-k-e two."

"Oh, no," came the yell from behind the backstop. "That one was outside!"

"Oh, but it wasn't!" I replied. "It was right down the pipe!"

Now they really started to get on Jerry's case for just watching the ball go by.

"Don't just stand there! Three called strikes is as bad as three swings and misses. You might as well at least TRY!"

Jerry now showed a renewed determination to get his bat on the ball. Giving his bat a couple of quick swings, he dug in, put his elbows up a notch and totally concentrated on the pitcher.

Merv again reared back for the third empty delivery. With a smooth motion he followed through down the front of the mound. As I was ready to "smack" my mitt again, I sensed a rush of air as Jerry put all of his weight into a hefty swing that split the cool night air across home plate.

"S-w-i-n-g and a miss! Strike three!"

Game over! Fryburg wins!

AFTER I READ this true story by Leroy Kuhns, I repeated it from the stage every now and then.

One night I was singing at an event, a benefit of some kind, at the Mt. Hope Auction, where they now have huge, new, beautiful Event Center buildings. I was singing from a stage under a tent, and between songs, someone yelled from the crowd, "Hey! Tell that baseball story!"

"It's your story," I countered, but the man yelled back, "Yeah, but you tell it better than we do."

Well, I don't think I tell it better than Leroy Kuhns, but I love the story and it always goes over well, so I began to tell it.

Abe Troyer was in the crowd near the back of the tent. Abe is a competitor, and he was one of the all-stars on the losing side of the now famous "invisible ball" ball game. He is now in a battery-powered wheelchair because he was paralyzed in a fall from an apple tree in his orchard 15 years or so ago.

As I began to tell the story, I noticed that Abe whipped his electric wheelchair around and motored out of the tent. He was not about to listen to this story!

Later that night when I was walking around the auction grounds, I saw Abe, so I stopped him and asked him, "Is that a true story, Abe? Did I tell it accurately?"

Abe is still a competitor. He looked all disgusted and he answered (disgustedly), "Oh... they exaggerate so bad!!" and he wheeled away.

A year or so later, I was in Pinecraft, Florida, singing at the Carnegie Hall of Pinecraft, Birky Square. I was just about to tell Leroy Kuhns's story when I saw Abe in the back of the crowd. I couldn't stand to see Abe get reminded of that humiliation again, so I quickly switched gears in the first sentence and told the Yost Hershberger baseball story from Chapter 5. Abe stayed and listened.

He enjoyed it.

~ 9

Three Up and Three Down!

ABE KNEPP WAS in Berlin to dedicate a bus that he had helped finance for The Gospel Express Prison Ministry. He flew up here in his own plane and brought a friend with him. I can't remember the friend's name.

I was having lunch with Abe and his friend at Boyd & Wurthmann Restaurant. In the course of the conversation, I told the Leroy Kuhns baseball story. Abe's friend then told another true baseball story:

SOMETHING SIMILAR HAPPENED in our community in West Virginia when I used to play softball. It was the last inning and it was dark, but the other team refused to consider the dangers of playing in the dark and insisted that we finish this last inning. They were behind and figured they could get a few runs in the dark.

We were at a terrible disadvantage, especially in the outfield. We could hardly see home plate from out there, it was so dark!

We outfielders got together and decided to each take a couple of softballs out with us. But it was so dark, we couldn't even throw the balls around the outfield while the pitcher was taking his warmup throws. The inning started and we could hear, but we couldn't see. We heard the crack of the bat, but we couldn't see anything.

Suddenly, *clunk.* A ball landed right close to me. I simply threw the extra ball that was in my glove into the infield. I didn't say a word. I just threw it in.

"One out," I heard the umpire yell.

Next batter. *Crack!*

Clunk. The left fielder threw in the ball that he was holding in his glove.

"Two outs. Next batter!"

We couldn't see each other grinning and smiling, but just then, *Crack!* Number three. *Clunk,* somewhere near me. I threw in the ball I was holding in my hand and jogged on in. Three up, three down. We won!

We all left the field in victory. Three balls lay somewhere out there in the outfield. I wonder if the next day in daylight, the home team would figure out they had been schnookered the night before.

~ 10

Duke Throws His Radio

BACK BEFORE DUKE joined the Amish Church, he and I played fast pitch softball on the same team in the Kidron League. He now owns a successful sawmill not far from the town of Fredericksburg.

Duke's wife was killed in a traffic accident, and not long after that, his daughter died in one of the most freakish tragedies in my recollection.

His daughter came home from a company Christmas banquet one night, but didn't come into the house. Duke finally went outside and saw her buggy and horse standing in the barnyard. He called her name. He looked around for her. Then he looked in the buggy, and it was empty! They eventually found her body, halfway up the lane. What had happened? Was it a stroke? A heart attack?

There was blood on top of her head, which was hard to see because it was dark. A bullet? A stone? They carried her into the house and called the sheriff's office. The sheriff came out and confirmed that it was a bullet wound. Someone had shot Duke's beautiful, innocent daughter. What in the world? Why? Who?

Word gets around in a small, close community and the next

day a neighbor who lives a mile down the road from Duke went to the sheriff.

"My son came home from deer hunting last night and discharged his muzzleloader in the air," he told the sheriff. "Could his bullet have traveled a mile and come down with enough velocity to kill someone?"

The sheriff did forensic work on the gun and the bullet, and sure enough, the boy hunter, who meant no harm, had unloaded his muzzleloader by shooting it in the air. A mile away, the bullet came down and went right through the buggy roof and into the girl's skull with enough velocity to kill her.

The boy got a very light punishment because of the quick confession, lack of intent, and the fact that Duke asked that no charges be filed. What's done is done. It was God's will (a very common Amish way of looking at tragedies and accidents).

I believe it was at his daughter's viewing that Duke and I got to talking and catching up. I had only seen him a few times in the years since we played softball. Of course, softball stories were told and slightly embellished. Today, many Amish youth have cell phones and devices to play music and listen to the Cleveland Indians, but in that particular church back then, transistor radios (remember them?) were strictly verboten (forbidden)!

But! That didn't mean that certain young Amish boys did not have one that they used to listen to the Cleveland Indians games and get some news from the outside world.

Duke was one of those certain boys. He had a radio that he kept well hidden upstairs. Here are two stories that he told me over the years:

On November 22, 1963, Duke was listening to his

contraband radio when he heard the awful news that the president of the United States had been shot. President Kennedy was dead! He couldn't believe it! And, although he could hardly contain this news, he dared not tell his dad, or Dad would wonder how he knew and the secret radio would be discovered. Duke told me that one of the hardest things he ever did was to keep this news to himself until his dad learned about Kennedy's assassination through a neighbor.

One night (June 19, 1970), Duke and his brothers were listening to the Cleveland Indians and pitcher Sonny Siebert had a no-hitter going against the New York Yankees. In the ninth inning, Horace Clarke, a relatively unknown Yankee, came up to the plate and smashed a single into left field, breaking up Siebert's no-hitter. Duke was so frustrated that he yelled and threw his radio, sending it crashing across the floor—and alerting his parents down below.

"Vas is am awh gehah? (What's going on?)" his dad yelled up the steps.

"Oh, nothing," Duke shouted down the stairs. "I just dropped something."

Horace Clarke not only broke up Sonny Siebert's no hitter, he was responsible for breaking up Duke's illegal radio.

~ 11

Chance(?) Encounter

IN THE LATE '60s, I stayed in a chicken coop in Pinecraft, Sarasota, Florida. The locals called it a house. They stretch the truth about other things, too.

Pinecraft is a small section of Sarasota occupied mostly by Amish and Mennonites who come to Florida during the winter. For six weeks, five of us Ohio boys stayed in one room of that "house." There was a bathroom, a shower, and running water… outside! You had to run and get it. And the water smelled like rotten eggs.

A young Amish couple from Pennsylvania stayed in the other side of the house. That's how we got to know John and Mary Fisher and their two young children, Steve and Lindy. We kept in touch with them for many years.

Fast forward 20 some years: Lindy is now in her late 20s and no longer Amish. She went to India as a missionary and, even though she never married, she adopted an Indian orphan.

In those 20 years, I got married and went to Costa Rica to work with youth during the '80s. We lived there for seven years. I had basically lost touch with the Fisher family except for newsletters and snippets of news from some friends we had in common. We returned home to the US in 1987 and got involved in a singing/prison ministry.

Four years ago, I went to a prison crusade in Pennsylvania where several hundred volunteers gathered at a church on Sunday afternoon for orientation. We were going to blitz every prison in Pennsylvania. After an afternoon of orientation and worship, all of us volunteers spread out to twenty-some prisons across the state.

When I got to my hotel 50 miles away, one of the volunteers told me that Lindy Fisher was also a volunteer and she had been at the orientation!

What? "Do you have her number?"

"Yes."

I called her. "Lindy! You're a part of this ministry?! I missed you! I didn't realize you were there!" She was at a women's prison somewhere else in Pennsylvania. We chatted for a few minutes and caught up with each other and her parents' and family's news.

So... The next year when I got to this same prison ministry, I called Lindy as soon as I got to the orientation session.

"Lindy, are you at the Prison Crusade this year?"

"No, I can't come this year. I'm in the process of adopting a child. In fact, I'm with the social worker right now."

Yes, she answered the phone even though she was in the middle of an adoption consultation. As we chatted, I heard the social worker interrupt her: "John? John who?"

Lindy said, "John Schmid. He's a friend who does prison ministry. He's from Ohio."

The social worker said, "John Schmid?! Give me that phone!"

The social worker grabbed Lindy's phone. "John! This is Sharon Buttemere!"

I was stunned. It took me a few seconds to process what had just happened. *Sharon Buttemere... Sharon Buttemere... Who?... Oh!*

"Sharon Buttemere! From Costa Rica! From our English-speaking youth group! But... I'm talking to an ex-Amish girl from Lancaster, PA..." I was amazed and confused and then delighted.

Amish Country in the US and Costa Rica are two different worlds, and although they are both part of my world, they are seldom (as in *never*) together.

Yes, that social worker living in Lancaster, PA, is a former member of our English-Speaking Youth Group in San Jose, Costa Rica, where she was born and raised by American missionary parents.

Sharon Buttemere (Sponsellor), whom I had known since she was around ten years old, was helping a former Amish girl who I have known since she was a baby, to adopt a child. What are the chances that the only person on the planet who would know both these ladies would call at the precise moment in time when both of them would for the first time (the only time?) be together?

Answer: The chances are one in a million.

Sharon and I chatted for several minutes, even though she was "on duty," and I told her I would be singing at a friend's front-yard concert in Lancaster County later that summer. She said she would come, and she did. She brought her retired missionary parents, and Lindy came with her parents, John and Mary Fisher. They all sat together on the lawn. I was friends with ALL of them! Parents, children, and now grandchildren.

We reconnected after almost 30 years.

What are the odds? Small world. A divine encounter!

~ 12

Outlaws, Contraband, and Amish Culture

This is taken from a story written by Ira Wagler and first published in 2007 on his blog, "Ira's Writings."

RECENTLY A FRIEND of mine told me about a conversation he had with his young teenage Amish neighbor. The Amish kid told him about all the contraband he had accumulated. An MP3 player that could store and play 1500 songs. A laptop computer with wireless card satellite internet access. And a cell phone, the kind you buy off the shelf with prepaid minutes. I asked my friend if the Amish kid's father knew of these things. He does not. A day of reckoning cometh. Sometime, somewhere, soon, it will all hit the fan. For both the kid and for the culture.

The young will defy and test the previous generation's boundaries and push them to the limits. It has always been so and will likely always be. This is particularly true in the Amish culture, with its austere lifestyle, where the rules prohibit all things modern, all things sinful such as music, radios, and television. And now the computer and the internet. Like my friend's neighbor, young people with a spark of life and an ounce of willpower simply will not accept their leaders' noble vacant admonitions forbidding the touching of "unclean things." Not without experimenting, experiencing, and deciding for themselves.

In my day, we were no different, only the technology was quite primitive. We thought we were really doing it with the little transistor radios. Available in various colors, with a little carry strap. AM and FM channels. Several of my older brothers had them even while we lived in Canada. We would huddle in the hayloft and listen to hockey games, always keeping a sharp lookout for Dad. My brother Steve listened live to the great Canadian-Russian hockey playoff in 1972, which Canada won in miraculous fashion in seven games.

I bought my first transistor radio in 1978, when I was sixteen, at Place's General Store on the west side of the square in Bloomfield. In a time before Walmart, Place's was our most convenient source of contraband, although we had to be very careful, as many other Amish also shopped there, and might witness our furtive purchases. And proclaim the news with great fanfare. Which would create a community-wide scandal. And wouldn't be good for anybody.

Other than newspapers and magazines, the little transistor radio was my first real window to the outside world. On it, I listened to country music, KWMT out of Fort Dodge, Iowa. 61 Country from Kansas City. 99 Country from Centerville. I hid my radio in the hay loft in the old west red horse barn and often listed for a few minutes when doing chores. Each radio came with a tiny ear plug, which transmitted tinny-sounding music. With this, I often listened late into the night while lying in bed. The old country singers still take me back to that time when I hear them. Johnny Cash. George Jones (who can still make me weep).

Haggard. Waylon and Willie. Tanya Tucker. Loretta Lynn. Crystal Gayle (whatever happened to her?). The Statler Brothers. The Oak Ridge Boys. And many, many others.

With the transistor radio, we became college football fans, cheering for the Hawkeyes. They were actually ranked in the top ten a few times back in those days. One of my most memorable football moments unfolded as I huddled behind our old white corn crib with my brother Nate on a fall Saturday afternoon, listening to the closing seconds of the Iowa-Michigan game, probably around 1982. Iowa kicked a field goal as time expired, winning 13-10. "The kick is up, it's on its way… IT'S GOOD!!!! IOWA WINS!!! IOWA WINS!!!" We danced and whooped and shouted like maniacs.

During the late 1970s, the 8-track tape player was cutting edge technology for our music. The gang of six guys I ran with had one or two among the lot. My best friend and future brother-in-law, Marvin, was very skilled and efficient in adapting the 8-track players to our large 12-volt buggy batteries. Marvin could also repair any torn tapes with glue and little bits of sticky tape.

Getting caught with such contraband had definite and potentially severe negative consequences. At the very least, whatever was found would be confiscated, and one would receive a good stiff bawling-out. And perhaps be grounded from going to the singing for a week or two. After we grew a bit older, the only negative was the disappearance of the radio or tape player. Once or twice, my transistor radio just disappeared. Nothing was ever said.

One night I got home very late, probably around 2 or 3 AM. I had the tape player in the buggy, and our collection of tapes. We kept them in a fifty-pound paper feed bag, Nutrena Feeds brand. It was so late and I was tired, so I did not hide the bag in the barn like I normally would have, and should have. Next morning after breakfast, when I reached into the back of the buggy to retrieve the bag, it was gone. Dad had been on the prowl bright and early.

He never said a word about it, just smiled a secret little smile. There were probably thirty or forty tapes in the bag, two or three hundred dollars' worth. An accumulation of much furtive buying and trading. Now reduced to ashes. I was highly irritated, furious, actually, but did not even bother to confront my father. Instead, the following week, I seized one of Dad's old shotguns, a Savage pump action 12-Gauge with a tendency to misfire. I trundled off with it to Jim's Auction House in town and sold it for $150. And kept the money. And smiled a secret smile. I figured we were about even.

And that's the way it went.

~ 13

Accidental Confession

A PLAIN CITY friend told this story (and I can't remember who):

Plain City used to be a thriving Amish community, until the mid-1970s when the Amish church either disbanded or the Amish moved to a different settlement. Yes, the Amish church simply disbanded! I had never heard of such a thing, but one Sunday the church was Amish; the next Sunday they were all Mennonites. You'll have to ask the locals for details.

Ben Miller (not his real name) was the local harness maker. His harness shop was also a community hangout, a gathering place for local farmers and friends to shoot the breeze, catch up on the local news, drink coffee…

One day, Ben discovered that a horse collar was missing. Stolen. He couldn't remember who had been in the shop that day or figure out when it went missing, but no one had been in the shop that he didn't know. Had someone broken in during the night? He had never noticed any signs of forced entry or any kind of disturbance among his wares.

A horse collar was no small item in Ben's harness shop inventory. Price-wise and hours of labor-wise, it was a significant loss.

Several years later, a local farmer we'll call "Mose" came in for some harness work, and while Ben was ringing up the bill, they chitchatted about the weather, the crops, the church...

During a lull in the conversation, the farmer asked, "Ben, did you ever find out who stole that horse collar?"

Ben stopped, turned around from the cash register, and leaned on the counter, looking at Mose for a few seconds. Then he spoke slowly and deliberately.

"Mose, I never told anyone about that stolen collar. Not even my wife! So, yes, I do believe I now know who stole it."

~ 14

The Sheriff Solves a Cold Case

(As told by David Kline)

HARRY WEISS WAS elected Holmes County Sheriff in 1935. Prior to that, Harry was the game warden in neighboring Tuscarawas County. It was in the early years of the Great Depression (1930?), and times were becoming hard. Families became desperate for money.

Trapping season opened on November 15, which was a Friday, and Game Warden Harry expected a lot of trappers would be out setting their traps on Saturday. But on the Monday before the 15th the game warden received a tip from a local resident that someone was already setting muskrat traps in Alpine Creek.

Harry had to check out the illegal trapper. Not even telling Edith, his wife, he left the house at midnight and drove to within half a mile of the creek, parked his car behind a copse of trees, and without any light, walked to the creek. Ever watchful, Harry walked as silently as a cat along the edge of the creek.

In some places Alpine Creek had pools up to six feet deep, while in other places it was fairly shallow. As he was sneaking along the edge of a deep pool, suddenly someone, or something, rushed out from the willow thicket and pushed Harry over the

65

edge into the water. The water was deep enough that Harry had to swim to shallower water. By then his assailant was long gone; he had melted into the cold dark night.

Giving up on apprehending the poacher, Harry hurried back to the car, went home, and changed into dry clothes. When he crawled into bed, he stayed away from Edith so she wouldn't detect his goosebumps. Harry told nobody what had transpired along Alpine Creek, soon after midnight on that cold November night. He didn't even tell Edith.

Years went by. Harry was elected Holmes County Sheriff in 1935, and the family moved to Walnut Creek Township. He served from 1935 to 1946, then again from 1957 to 1961. His last term was from 1965 to 1967, when his son Darryl replaced him.

It was likely in the early 1940s when the rest of this story took place:

A Tuscarawas man about Harry's age was a fire extinguisher salesman, well known to the local community, and a fine storyteller besides. I'm not sure what the offence was, but Shorty ended up in the crossbar motel (ahem... the jail), and while there, he had somewhat of a conversion experience. The hellfire-and-brimstone prison preacher convinced Shorty that he should amend his dodgy ways and make things right with folks he had wronged.

Upon his release from the pen, Shorty went back on the road with his fire extinguisher job, and one of his stops was the Holmes County jail in Millersburg. Sure enough, the sheriff was at his desk when Shorty stopped in. After a few minutes of chitchat on the local scene in the familiar Pennsylvania Dutch dialect, Shorty asked the sheriff, "Do you remember when you were the game warden in the next county, and one night someone pushed you into the creek?"

Harry didn't say a word. He stood up to his full 5' 8," cocked his arm, and punched Shorty, whose 6' 4" frame towered over the sheriff, right on the chin.

Shorty was startled as he fell backwards. "Oww, that hurt!" he moaned.

"That water was cold!" said Sheriff Harry.

~ 15

"Ich bin da Harry Weiss!"

HARRY WEISS WAS my sister-in-law's grandfather and her dad was Darryl Weiss. Both men were Holmes County sheriffs in their day. They were born-and-bred Holmes County Swiss, and they both spoke the Pennsylvania Dutch dialect, which made them well-liked and well-received among the Amish.

Marvin J. Miller shared this Harry Weiss story with me:

In the mid-1960s, new laws were passed concerning horse-drawn vehicles. The Amish were required to have certain lighting and reflector tape on their buggies or they were not legal after dark. Most of the Amish complied immediately, not only because they are usually obedient to authority, but for their own safety as well. Traffic was getting heavier and faster in sleepy Holmes County. As in any group, there were those who resisted because they didn't like change, they thought it was against their conscience, or maybe they were just slightly lazy.

One evening just a little past twilight, Sheriff Harry Weiss saw Amishman Noah Kauffman traveling through Berlin with no lights on his buggy. It not only was illegal, it was dangerous for a black buggy driving in the dark night. It could have been hit by a truck.

Harry jumped in his cruiser and followed the buggy for a quarter mile or so with his cruiser lights flashing, but the horse didn't even break stride. It just kept clopping down the road at a pretty brisk clip.

Maybe the driver couldn't see the lights? Maybe he was asleep? Why didn't he stop?

Harry followed the buggy with his lights flashing for a reasonable time, and then he got on his vehicle's "bullhorn" loudspeaker, which was quite an innovation at that time. *I'll get his attention,* Harry thought.

In a clear, loud, and perfect Pennsylvania Dutch, he broadcast a message loud enough to be heard halfway to the Goose Bottom Valley: "ICH BIN DA SHERIFF WEISS! SCHTOPE!" ("I am Sheriff Weiss! Stop!")

The Amishman, surprised but not rattled, stuck his head out the side of the buggy and looked back at Harry. Without taking his hands off the reins or slowing down one bit, he answered, "ICH BIN DA NOAH KAUFFMAN! GIDDYUP!" ("I am Noah Kauffman! Giddyup!")

~ 16

"I Wore Gloves!"

ELI HERSHBERGER WAS Lydia's second cousin. He was developmentally disabled, a condition thought to be caused by a vaccination when he was young. Eli imagined that he was a cowboy, and the Amish church looked the other way when he wore non-approved cowboy boots instead of lace-up work shoes. And they allowed him to wear a cowboy hat instead of a regular black Amish hat with a straight 2 ¾-inch brim. In fact, the church was lax on quite a few rules for Eli. They knew his condition wasn't his fault.

Eli was a friend of mine. If you would meet him, it might take several minutes for you to realize that he was not like other folks. Several times he invited me to a fish fry after he had been to Lake Erie the day before. "And bring your guitar!"

Eli could hold a simple job, but every now and then he would just wander off, both mentally and physically, and not be concerned at all about his responsibilities. I wonder if that is what happened at his job at the Barr boys' pallet shop in Maysville.

Eli got fired.

The Barr boys were sort of a rough bunch. Lydia remembers the time they came into the Byler home late one Halloween night

71

and dumped her brothers' beds upside down and left like a band of outlaws. She and her sisters hid under the covers, shivering in terror. Overall, the Barr boys were a fun-loving, crazy gang, although some of their dealings in lumber and timber were sometimes suspect.

The morning after Eli was fired, the Barr Pallet Shop fired up for another productive day, but something was wrong. Nothing worked! It didn't take a Sherlock Holmes or an engineer to discover the problem. All the belts had been greased. Someone had purposely put grease on all the belts so that when the motor started, every belt slipped!

Again, it didn't take an FBI agent to suspect who might have done this. They went to Eli to question him.

"Eli, you greased our belts, didn't you?"

"Nope!"

"Eli, we know you did it!"

"Nope!"

"We have proof!" (Which was not true. They were just highly suspicious.)

Eli was resolute: "Nope!"

"We found fingerprints!"

Eli: "Nope! You couldn't have! I wore gloves!"

So... with no proof (no fingerprints and no cameras in those days), the Barr Boys had no choice but to drop the case.

~ 17

Highway (Township Road) Robbery

AT THE LOCAL Boyd & Wurthmann coffee shop in Berlin, where many problems in America are solved and many others are created, those of us at the Table of Knowledge and Wisdom were discussing the death of a well-known local preacher named Urie Shetler. Urie was my father-in-law's cousin. His nephew, Vern Shetler, was also at the table. (In Amish Country, everybody is related.)

We were discussing Urie's life and his dramatic conversion to Christ. Urie was a tough, rebellious Amish boy who ran away from home in his late teens and joined a gang in Wooster, not quite fifteen miles away. I've never lived in Wooster, although our address for most of my life was R.D.#4, Wooster. I didn't know Wooster was big enough to have gangs. I guess gangs don't have size requirements for their host cities.

Part of the initiation for the gang that Urie joined was to rob an Amish buggy. Well, not the buggy, but the Amish person in the buggy.

I'm not sure about the robbing part, but the Amish part was right down Urie's alley. He had grown up in Amish Country. He knew the Amish community fairly well. In fact, he had grown up

STORIES FROM AMISH COUNTRY

Amish! The gang members and Urie got in their car and headed for Holmes County.

I'm guessing it was a weekend because the buggy they stopped was driven by two young teenage boys. That would mean that they were probably on their way to see their girlfriends. Or they were on their way home from a date.

The gang members jumped out of their car and grabbed the reins of the horse. Urie pointed a gun at the freaked-out boys and said, "Give me your money!" The two boys handed their wallets to Urie.

This crazy, almost unbelievable story about a very conservative, faithful Mennonite preacher, whose reputation as a fiery, fearless proclaimer of Christ's love was well known, almost nationwide among the plain communities. As the account was being told one more time that morning, one of the men at the table said, "Yes, that's a true story. That was my dad's buggy! He robbed my dad!"

We all looked at Nelson Miller, and he went on to explain: "My dad (Dickey Monroe's Jr.) and Bert Beachy were driving down the road and were stopped by three tough-looking guys. One of them had a gun, and he pointed it at my dad and said, 'Give me all your money.'"

Unfortunately for Urie, these Amish boys recognized him! Nelson's dad said, "Urie! Du vaisht bessah as dess!" ("Urie! You know better than this!") Urie's career as a robber was in serious jeopardy. Robbers don't wear masks because of pandemics. They wear them so they won't be recognized. Urie was busted!

Because these boys knew who it was that had robbed them, it took about one day for the police to identify and arrest Urie. His tenure as a member of a Wooster gang lasted less than one week. He was sent to prison for three years. I don't know the details of his Christian conversion, but I'm guessing three years in the slammer gave him time to think and mend his ways, which he did.

As we at the morning-coffee table contemplated the severity and foolishness of this story and thought about what actually could have happened, Nelson said, "When my dad and Bert handed over their wallets, Dad told Urie to take the money but please give the wallet back. He had a picture of his girlfriend in it."

Jr. and Bert did get their wallets and the pictures back, but laughter erupted over our coffee cups when Nelson told "the rest of the story"—

His dad later told his family, "I was so ashamed. *I only had three dollars!*"

How embarrassing! And how is a hard-working robber supposed to make it on those kinds of wages?

~ 18

A Shot in the Dark

(As told by David Kline)

OLD BEN SPEELMAN did not like people hunting on his land. He let it be known that he would shoot any trespasser.

Hans Yoder, Jerry Kline, and Vernon Kline were coon hunting one cool night on the farm adjacent to the Speelman farm. It was about midnight, and they hadn't had much luck. The dogs had run into a cold trail; the coon had outsmarted the dogs and was probably up in a tree, out of breath, and looking down with a smile on the confused dogs and the bored men.

While the men were standing around shooting the breeze and trying to get the dogs to come out of the woods, Hans reached into his hunting jacket and pulled out his smoke pipe. Then he reached into the pocket again and got a handful of pipe tobacco and proceeded to expertly pack it into his pipe. His experienced thumb pressed down several times and then took one more pinch of tobacco from the coat pocket. Then he lit the pipe and started puffing while he listened to his friends tell stories of hunts gone by.

In the coolness and quietness of the night, with the aroma

of pipe tobacco in the air, all of a sudden, *BLAM!*, A gunshot blast! And Hans's hat flew up in the air.

Hans held his face with a look of terror and all four startled men ran for their lives in four different directions. The dogs started barking and running toward the direction of the gunshot, figuring that they were missing out on a coon. Old Ben Speelman must have thought they were on his land, even though they were a good hundred yards from his line fence.

Hard to tell how far they ran and how much time elapsed, but after a while, all the men were somewhere in the dark, panting and keeping deathly quiet, waiting for the next shot.

In the darkness, separated, they each stood silent for a few minutes, trying to assess the situation. The dogs came running in from several directions and looked around, confused, wondering where the coon was.

When they slowly wandered back through the dark and found each other, they stood around and wondered what to do next. Why would old Ben shoot when they were clearly not on his land?

Hans put his pipe back in his mouth and took a slow long puff. But there was no puff. No smoke. He looked at his pipe with his flashlight. There was no tobacco in it. In fact, it was as clean as a brand-new pipe! What in the world?

Then Hans realized his face was peppered with gunpowder and pipe tobacco. How had that happened?

After some talk and discussion and the fact that Ben Speelman did not come out of the woods with more warnings, they began to piece together what had happened: When Hans reached into his coat pocket, he also got a .22 caliber round of ammo and packed it into his pipe with the tobacco. When the good-smelling tobacco burned down to the bullet, it got hot, exploded, and blew up through the "barrel" of his pipe and through his hat and peppered his face with tobacco and gunpowder!

Since the dogs were all gathered in and they were now physically and emotionally exhausted, they decided to pack it in and head home. It wasn't Ben Speelman after all, but a stray bullet planted by Hans himself.

I never heard what happened after that, but I am guessing that Hans Yoder was a lot more careful when he packed tobacco in his pipe. Always check for .22 bullets. They are hard on hats. And pipes. And hearts.

~ 19

Plowing on a Sunday

My MOTHER-IN-LAW'S FAMILY is from Buchanan County, Iowa, a very strict Amish settlement. Tobe Byler went out to Iowa from Ohio in the early '40s and married Amelia Gingerich. They lived in Iowa the first three years of their marriage and then moved back to Wayne County, Ohio, in time for my wife, Lydia, to be born a Buckeye.

One day in our church several years ago, Laura Gingerich Mast, one of Lydia's cousins (one of hundreds, if you also count second cousins) told me a story from her family. She got it from her dad, Dan Gingerich, and she told it to me, so it's been handed down over the years, traveling through several people, a couple of generations, from three states away. Since I couldn't remember all the details, I called Laura, and then I called Linda, her mom. I discovered that they didn't remember all the details either. Linda couldn't remember the year this happened, but she said it happened a long time ago, while Dan, her future husband, was still at home. I know that several years ago Linda saw some of the neighbors who were involved in this story but not a word was said about it. You will see why.

So here's the story in my words, and I'm sticking to it. You'll see that any details I might have made up don't take away from the heart of what really happened.

Fred Gingerich, Dan's father, farmed 400 acres, which is huge for an Amish farmer who uses only horses. No tractors. He also had a large number of horses. His friends and cousins told me he had 40 horses! Those horses could do a heap of work, but feeding and caring for that many animals is a big job in itself.

Fred was a diligent farmer, always on time with plowing, cultivating, planting, harvesting, milking. His crops showed it, and his horses (and his buggy) always looked like they were ready to show at the county fair. That is, if Amish were allowed to attend the fair. Which they are not.

That year Iowa had a very wet spring. The Gingerichs were way behind in their plowing. And just about the time they could get the ploughs into the drying fields, it was Sunday, with rain threatening again on Monday. That would set them back another several days, maybe a week.

If corn is planted late, there are several things that can go wrong. There is a risk of a killing frost before the corn is mature (if it's planted on time, it isn't out of the ground yet when it frosts). There's also a risk of bugs and pests getting into the stalks and the ears. A bunch of things can go wrong for late-planted corn, and the yield can be reduced by two bushels an acre. In other words, delayed planting is trouble for a diligent farmer. (It's trouble for the bad farmer, too. He just doesn't worry about it.)

Farming is risky enough when the weather is perfect. And when a farmer like Dan's dad gets behind in his work, he is three times as stressed as us normal people would be. Fred was stressed.

It was a beautiful Sunday morning when the family hitched up to go to church. I have been to Buchanan County to visit Lydia's uncles, and I know that the Amish families out there can be spread out, so it's very possible that church that morning was at least a half hour away by buggy.

I'm imagining Fred looking out the front of the buggy at the unplowed field as they left for church, scanning the perfect blue skies, and thinking about how much could be plowed that day. Then he looked at the calendar which said "Sabbath." Plowing on a Sunday was not even in his remotest thoughts, but he was just hoping the weather forecast for the next day was wrong and Monday would be as perfect as it was that Sunday morning.

A good team can plow about two acres a day, and they had a lot more than two acres to plow and not much time to plow it. How would they get the crops in?

Church was at a relative's house that day. (How do I know that? They're all related!) The preachers preached for around three hours, and then the deacons gave testimony. The closing prayers were said and the meal was served. There was good conversation around the table. Although some Amish churches don't sit around a table for lunch. They stand around it and then they move to make way for the next group. But I digress.

The Gingerichs hitched up to return home for a nap before evening chores. Fred was snoozing on and off, listening to the rhythm of the *clop, clop* of the buggy horse, who didn't need any encouraging to hurry home or any instructions on how to get there. Horses know their way home. These new "hands-free" driving cars, "Technology That Drives Confidence," are not really new. They have nothing on the generations-old horse and buggy, especially when the horse knows he is on his way home. Travel is "hands free." Take a nap.

As they approached the home place, Fred woke up, focused his eyes on his fields, and thought he was dreaming.

What in the world? He thought it looked like... like his fields were plowed! He blinked and looked again. He looked around. Where was he? Yes, they were approaching home, and yes, these were his fields. *But they are plowed! I swear they look plowed! How can this be?*

The Gingerich family stared at each other in disbelief. Yes, Dad saw it, too. The children saw it. They were not hallucinating. The fields were PLOWED!

They unhitched, put the horse in the barn, walked around, scratched their heads. The fields were plowed! It messed up their nap. How in the world can you sleep when acres of fields get plowed while you are in church? On a Sunday!

Laura told me that nobody said a word. The Amish preachers didn't ask any questions. The Gingerichs said nothing. Not one of the neighbors acted like anything had happened. From what I know, Fred Gingerich's crops were put in on time, cultivated, harvested, and sold or fed to the livestock like nothing had happened. Like the weather had been perfect.

Dan and Linda Hostetler Gingerich were married in 1962, and this story happened before they were married, so it is at least 65 years old, and I hear it still gets told in Buchanan County and Gingerich family circles. Always with a smile.

EXPLANATION: The neighbors saw the Gingerichs' dilemma and decided to help. They all got together with their tractors and plows and waited until the Gingerichs' buggy was down the road and out of sight, and then they cranked up their tractors and one by one, out of each barn or shed came John Deeres, Internationals, Ford Fergusons, Cases... and they came to the Gingerich Amish farm (on a Sunday!) and plowed over 40 acres before the second Amish preacher would have sat down in church.

Laura told me that none of the neighbors said a word and the Gingerichs never asked any questions. I'm guessing that there was a new, deeper appreciation for the non-Amish neighbors, and vice versa.

Now folks, I'm with the Amish when it comes to working on a Sunday. It should be a day of rest. *Remember the Sabbath and keep it holy* (Exodus 20:8).

But I can't help but think that God looked down on all those tractors working on Sunday, and He smiled. I can hear Him up there in Heaven, saying, "Hey Gabriel, come over here! Take a look at this!"

Gabriel came over, looked down, saw those farmers working (ahem, "helping a neighbor") on the Sabbath, and he also couldn't help but smile. "Those English people! What are we going to do with them?"

"It is lawful to do good on the Sabbath"
- Jesus, Matthew 12:12

Other books by John Schmid:

Encounters: In and Out of Prison with John Schmid
Go behind the scenes (and the prison bars) with John and get a glimpse of the highs and lows of a life committed to the service of God and man.
Available on Amazon or from John Schmid

Showing Up: I Was in Prison and You Visited Me
Hard work, heat, bugs, boarding with local families, language barriers, frustration, satisfaction, rewards... The challenges and blessings of a life dedicated to both a prison ministry and raising a family.
Available on Amazon or from John Schmid

The Power of a Song: How a Song Changed Everything
A collection of stories about the influence a song can have on a person, a crowd, or a culture.
Available on Amazon or from John Schmid

Songs in Dutch, With English Translations
A compilation of side-by-side English and Dutch renditions of songs sung by John.
Available from John Schmid

For a list of John's CDs, see next page --

John Schmid CDs:

Text 330-231-1164 or email johnschmid89@gmail.com to order

With Love, Country
Common Ground
Maximum Security
Greystone Chapel
At Christmastime
Backstage
This Is My Father's World
Everybody Needs Jesus
Golden Love
Acoustic
I Walked Where Jesus Walked
In Dutch
What a Time!
In Dutch, Again!
Almost Bluegrass
Final Destination
Dutch Blitz
A Tribute to Johnny Cash
The Church in The Wildwood
Plain Fun
A Country Christmastime
A Christmas Concert
Home
From The Cash Cabin to Baker's Barn
The Ballad of Jacob Hochstetler

Made in the USA
Columbia, SC
22 June 2024